Every emotion has a story

AF669467

Tori DeShields

BookLeaf Publishing

Presentation by *BookLeaf Publishing*

Web: www.bookleafpub.com

E-mail: info@bookleafpub.com

ISBN: 9789357616942

First edition 2022

Hey Gram. . . This one's for you!

Please continue to be there for me, and I thank you for always supporting me. I love you so much! Don't worry, I'm just getting started.

Samya, this is your sign to always follow your dreams. I will forever support you! I love you!

ACKNOWLEDGEMENT

I want to thank my past, present, and preparation for the future.
Every heartbreak, every smile, every revelation all contributed to my first step to something bigger

PREFACE

I had so much joy creating this piece together. For you to read from my past to my present. . Preparing for the future. My only goal is to touch someone's soul. If I can help someone be honest to themselves and give them the confidence to express their emotions, I did what I was supposed to do with this book

Prayer

Heavenly spirit, Arc Angel Micheal, and to my
divine angels above
I Thank you for protecting me
Always, with so much love

I Thank you for guiding me everyday
I Thank you for showing me my divine way

I ask that you continue to protect and heal me to
my purpose of life
Because without your love, support and
guidance, I would be repeating a dangerous
cycle twice.

Asé

Whistle In The Fall

Feeling the breeze through the trees
Hitting my ears
Humming with possibilities

Feeing free
Hearing the crows caw
While walking deeper through the neighborhood

Laughing with joy
While the orange leaves sway to the ground
The wind whooshing louder than the car

The animals frolic through the freshly cut grass.
All in one amazing afternoon
Deep breath
Smile
Grateful

Bebita

You say this and that
I want to believe you
but it is so hard to when you don't do what you
say you're going to do

You have a list of ideas
a mind with the wild imagination, dreams galore
But such a lack of determination

Now self, bebita, I don't mean to be hard on you
that is never my intention,
but it is time to get focused
if happiness is your next direction

Did I mention how proud of you I am? You have
come such a long way every step is progress
And be sure to show gratitude each day

Trust - The firm belief in the reliability of
someone or something
I want you to have this for you because it's time
for you to be bigger and do what you say you're
going to do

Let’s Do It

I no longer just want to just exist
Lacking drive; falling into a depressive abyss.
My dream is to twirl with the increased feeling of bliss
New beginnings, the past will only be missed

It’s time to move forward
*blows kiss

Untitled

Beautiful. Sexy. Mysterious.
An open book, but so many pages stuck together. . .
Those are the details you keep hidden. Deeply hidden.
Until the right reader comes along . . . Mystical forever

Is Self Love Enough?

Is self love enough
Because the love of another I crave
But the more this is promoted
It seems all the rave

Growing up, you can say I was looking for love
in all the wrong places
mesmerized by their smiles
ignoring the lies written on their faces

Only focusing on the compliments given
about my body, my hips, and my smile
after that exchange
I wonder why I'm sitting here alone for a while

There's absolutely no shame in wanting love
but self-love helps the good attract because
when the wrong ones proceed towards you
you will be easily able to subtract

Is self-love enough?
to some it is, and to others it's not
but before you go looking for a new partner
make sure you love yourself a whole lot

How Much?

How much love can you give?
It was one date and done
I guess that was fun
And that's why I had to change the narrative

Dear Darkness

Dear Darkness,

211 is displayed next to a memory of you.
I fight the feeling
But, it's not the fact that I'm thinking of you. It's not the fact that I desire to be with you.
It's the fact that it's time. It's time to share my story.

I Preach

I preach emotion because I am full of expression. I believe that life can cause a person to experience any and every emotion possible. Even feeling something that you made up; 100% self made, possible! If it takes over your soul and your mind, it's an emotion and you can feel it.

I have so much bark, I don't allow myself to be exposed to bitting. It's not my character.

Today, I was reminded of the bark I sang about the immature creature. Questioning why I was allowing Myself to be subjected to the same environment as the creature that I despised. And the only answer that I could find was that the task at hand was what I most enjoyed, not the creature. The task at hand I was able to be myself, perform my best abilities, and gain new responsibilities that I enjoyed practicing daily. Immature creature and The subjects that surrounded her, would not take advantage of my happiness at hand. They would not be the reason for choosing to revoke my passions and talents.

Manifest

Manifesting - to take our thoughts and ideas and turn them into reality

The frustration you feel
That your "manifestations" must be blurred,
Others dreams are coming true
making you feel like you're being unheard.

Please do not compare yourself
Even though the saying it's easier said than done,
Multiples; left and right
And you're looking for just one.

Spiritual Manifestation
Let's put the work in, make those dreams come true,
The universe May have the last word
but it cannot start without you!

Realization

Today I realized it has to stop.
Stop fantasizing what could be.
Stop imagining what you wanted.
Because we can no longer hold on to what we
have created in our mind. And need to let go.
Accept what's in your face.

I am worthy
I am valuable
I am the prize.

Healing

Healing and wholeness has to come from the inside.
Time cannot heal all wounds, but all wounds can heal in time.

I Refuse

Over criticizing caused discouragement
Pushing me closer to ending my commitment.
No doubt that I give my all through and through.
I will not throw my love just because of you.
I refuse to let you ruin my enjoyment

Emotions

Everyday my emotions fluctuate
They never stay in a constant state
Either up or down
Causing happiness or frown
They always tend to circulate.

Ability To Trust

And after all I put you through
Scrambled, heartbroken; what to do
Staring at the openness in trees
Begging my higher self please
Because all I wanna do is trust you.

Taste of The Journey

Oh honey, they lied when they said the healing journey was fun
It feels like constant down pour, this ain't no walk in the sun.

Be Open

You don't have to keep going at this alone, you
know
Be open to receiving love and just go with the
flow
I promise you will not have to feel the feeling of
shutting down
Because this is your divine partner; support has
truly been found

Ready

Looking for guidance to show me where I
belong
I am truly hesitant in making my decisions both
right and wrong
I am ready to live abundantly
On a journey to purposely be me
I am grateful, but this journey is taking so long

Patience ✨

Arrangement

With you, things feel so natural and clear
Even with clouded thoughts, it feels like clarity
is near
Like the universe orchestrated this arrangement.
In our present talking about an engagement.
I have faith that this positivity will block this
deep rooted fear.

Book on The Shelf

You were a beautiful Novel
I will cherish the pages
Maybe memories a few sentences for laughs
But I can no longer bend the corners for comfort
I am proud of all the creativity used in our story
But it's time for a new.

Just one

Your thoughts are all over the place
All you need to do is write it down
Just put the pen to the piece of paper
You don't have to speak, no sound

What needs to be understood,
Where all you need to do is start,
Because if it's pondering in your mind so much
Then it just has to be heavy on your heart

You may still be struggling about your future
and your passions
But I Love that you are watching your feelings
about the things you can't control
But it's time to put focus forth the things you
enjoy
The things that are connected to your soul

You loved writing stories when you were young
Why did you let that go?
And poetry, oh you loved poetry
Just write one - the world needs to know.

You are such a magical being
Just start and write one,

Now that your first poem is completed
The hardest part is done

I love you.

www.ingramcontent.com/pod-product-compliance
Lightning Source LLC
Chambersburg PA
CBHW062205160726
48282CB00027B/1007
* 9 7 8 9 3 5 7 6 1 6 9 4 2 *